This belongs to

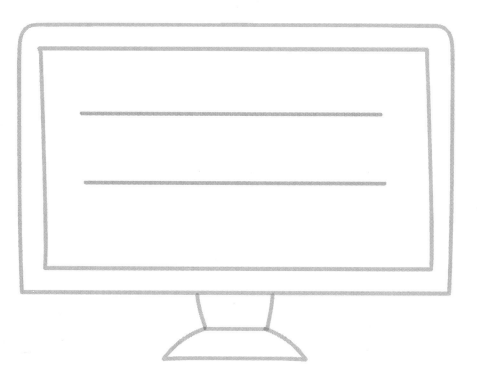

I'm a teacher.
To save time,
let's just
assume I'm
always right.

Made in United States
Orlando, FL
02 November 2021

10157653R00057

Create Your Dream Life Now

A Workbook & Guide for Manifesting Your Destiny

Written by Darren Marc
Illustrated by Joan Coleman

**Library of Congress Cataloging-in-Publication Data
is available through the Library of Congress**

© 2018 Darren Marc and Joan Coleman

ISBN-13: 978-07573-2101-6(Paperback)
ISBN-10: 07573-2101-1(Paperback)
ISBN-13: 978-07573-2102-3 (ePub)
ISBN-10: 07573-2102-X(ePub)

Publisher: Health Communications, Inc.
3201 S.W. 15th Street
Deerfield Beach, FL 33442–8190

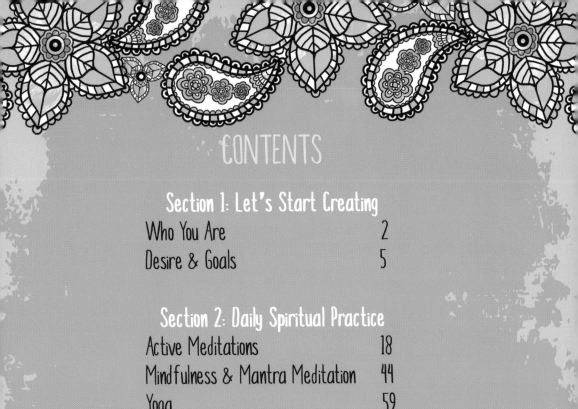

CONTENTS

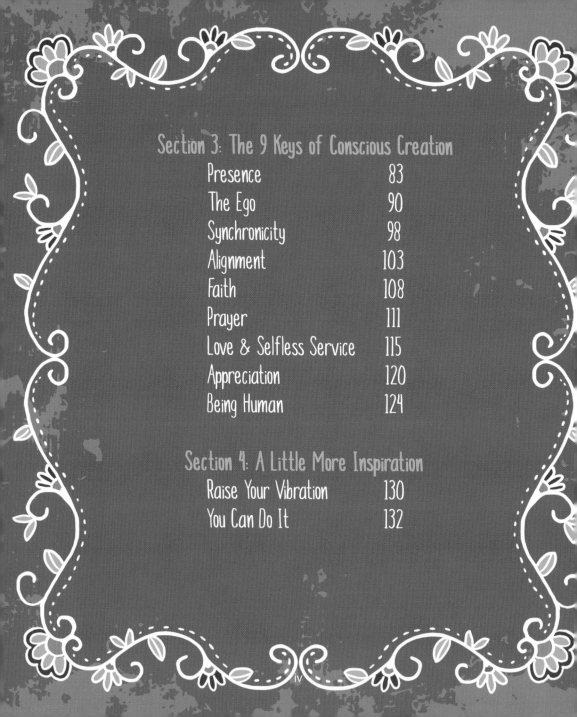

A NOTE FROM THE AUTHOR

We all have an inner light that was created to shine brightly in the world. It is our true self, which embodies peace, love, happiness, joy, abundance, and well-being on all levels. The exercises and tools in this book are designed to be fun, to help you connect to that aspect of your being, and to create a life you love living.

To get the most from this book, I suggest that you explore it from start to finish. Workbook pages are scattered throughout, and I encourage you to take your time completing them. If you sense you are losing presence and focus, it's perfectly fine to put the book down and return to it another time. You might want to have a journal beside you for extra writing space when needed.

Once your daily spiritual practice is in place, and you're rocking your healthy living habits and daily rituals, return to the 9 keys of conscious creation whenever you need to for inspiration and support. Most importantly, HAVE FUN!

If you'd like to share your workbook pages with me and the world, e-mail them to CYDLNow@Gmail.com and I will post them on my Instagram and Facebook pages. More information and resources are available at: www.awakenwithdarren.com.

Much Love to All, Darren

Section 1:
Let's Start
Creating

WHO YOU ARE

You are an aspect of source, the same energy that created the sun, the stars, the moon, and the entire universe! As an aspect of source, you are a powerful, creative being.

Everything that exists as form in the universe once existed as a possibility in an infinite field of potentiality. Your dreams reside in this infinite field. You can birth them into creation, and it all begins with desire.

You project your thoughts, vision, feelings, and belief systems out into the universe with inspired action, and the universe reflects that back to you as your life. You are literally writing your own movie, and you are the star!

DESIRE

Desire is everything.

It is the spark of creation.

A SMART goal is specific, measurable, attainable, relevant (aligned with your life's intention), and time bound. On the following pages, write down all the SMART goals you want to manifest within the next six months. Beneath each goal, write down two actions steps you can take within the next 30 days to help you achieve the goal.

Personal Development

What goals do you have related to improving
yourself and becoming a better person?

_____
_____
_____
_____
_____
_____
_____
_____
_____
_____
_____
_____
_____
_____
_____
_____
_____
_____

Health

What goals do you have related to feeling totally amazing in your body?

_____

_____

_____

_____

_____

_____

_____

_____

_____

_____

_____

_____

_____

_____

_____

_____

Family & Romance

What goals do you have related to family, love, and romance? These goals can include dreams related to a current partnership or one you wish to create.

_____

_____

_____

_____

_____

_____

_____

_____

_____

_____

_____

_____

_____

_____

_____

_____

Fun

What are some of your fun goals? Think about the things in life that bring you the most joy!

Career

What are your career goals? These goals can be related to a current career or a new area you want to explore.

_____

_____

_____

_____

_____

_____

_____

_____

_____

_____

_____

_____

_____

_____

_____

_____

_____

_____

Finance

What are your financial goals?
Be as specific as possible!

_____
_____
_____
_____
_____
_____
_____
_____
_____
_____
_____
_____
_____
_____

Spirituality

Do you have any goals related to your spiritual life? If so, what are they?

_____

_____

_____

_____

_____

_____

_____

_____

_____

_____

_____

_____

_____

_____

_____

FUN EXERCISE

Utilizing a poster board or bulletin board, create a vision board with one or two images to represent each of your goals. Place your vision board in a place where you can easily see it every day. It will help you to concentrate and maintain focus on your most meaningful goals!

FUN EXERCISE 2

Join the private Facebook group "Create Your Dream Life Now." Post your goals and find a new friend to be your accountability partner. Chat with your new friend once a week for at least 10 minutes to support each other with your goals, daily spiritual practice, and healthy living habits.

Section 2:
Daily Spiritual Practice

ACTIVE MEDITATIONS

These 7 active meditations utilize the power of your heart-centered awareness to bring you into alignment with the beauty of the present moment and your dreams. Explore one or two meditations a day for 10 to 20 minutes each. Later, you'll get to choose your favorites to include in a daily spiritual practice routine.

1. GRATITUDE FOR THE NOW

Gratitude boosts the feel-good neurotransmitters dopamine and serotonin. If you want to start feeling good, and attracting more things to be grateful for in your life, giving thanks for what you have now is the best way to start.

Gratitude

Write down 10 things you
are grateful for today.

I am so happy and grateful for:

1. _____

2. _____

3. _____

4. _____

5. _____

6. _____

7. _____

8. _____

9. _____

10. _____

The Meditation

1. Find a comfortable seat and close your eyes.

2. Place your hands together in front of your heart center.

3. Observe the natural rhythm of your breath for a minute or two.

4. Silently whisper an affirmation to yourself for something you are grateful for in the present moment, such as "I am so happy and grateful for [fill in what you are thankful for here]." Use the list you've just created as inspiration, and think of as many things as possible.

   ADVANCED PRACTICE: After you leave your house, do this gratitude meditation continuously for the first hour of your day (with eyes open, of course!).

2. GRATITUDE FOR THE FUTURE

By giving thanks for what you want as if you have it now, you raise your personal frequency to match the frequency of that which you seek. When you do that, magic will start to unfold in your life!

Gratitude

Write down 10 things you want. Be grateful for them as if you have them now.

I am so happy and grateful for:

1. _____

2. _____

3. _____

4. _____

5. _____

6. _____

7. _____

8. _____

9. _____

10. _____

The Meditation

1. Find a comfortable seat and close your eyes.

2. Observe the natural rhythm of your breath for a minute or two.

3. Place your hands together in front of your heart center.

4. Silently whisper an affirmation to yourself for something you want as if you have it now. For example, let's say you want to attract a new romantic partner. You might silently whisper, "I am so happy and grateful for the beautiful, spiritual partner in my life who fulfills all of my wants and needs." Use the list you just created as inspiration and think of as many things as possible.

   HELPFUL TIP: You can also explore this meditation lying down! Close your eyes, make yourself comfortable, and spend 10 to 15 minutes immersed in the life you want to be living 6 or 12 months from now.

3. AFFIRMATIVE PRAYER

If you want to fulfill the desires of your heart, your thoughts, belief systems, and actions need to be in alignment with what you want.

25

Negative thoughts and old belief systems can
be transformed into positive thoughts and
new belief systems with the power of
affirmative prayer.

I AM is another name for source.
By repeating the words I AM, you
are invoking your power as a
co-creator with source in oneness
with that which you are.

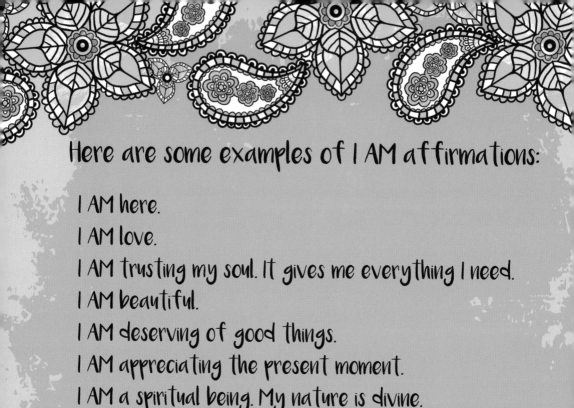

Here are some examples of I AM affirmations:

I AM here.
I AM love.
I AM trusting my soul. It gives me everything I need.
I AM beautiful.
I AM deserving of good things.
I AM appreciating the present moment.
I AM a spiritual being. My nature is divine.
I AM guided every step by Spirit who leads me
    toward what I must know and do.
I AM an open channel for creative ideas.
I AM at peace with all that has happened, is
    happening, and will happen.

Affirmations

Create 10 *I AM* affirmative prayers
that are reflective of your goals.

I AM _____

I AM _____

I AM _____

I AM _____

I AM _____

I AM_____

I AM _____

I AM _____

I AM _____

I AM _____

The Meditation

1. Find a comfortable seat and close your eyes.
2. Place your hands together in front of your heart center.
3. Observe the natural rhythm of your breath for a minute or two.
4. Silently repeat as many affirmative prayers as you'd like!

ADVANCED PRACTICE: Every time you catch yourself having a negative thought about yourself or your life, replace it with an affirmative prayer!

4. CREATIVE VISUALIZATION

Creative visualization is a powerful technique that uses your imagination to help make goals and dreams come true. As Oprah Winfrey said, "If you can see it and believe it, it is a lot easier to achieve it." Famous athletes, CEOs, and celebrity actors have all used creative visualization to fuel their success and you can too!

The Meditation

1. Find a comfortable seat and close your eyes.

2. Imagine yourself experiencing what you want as if you have it now. Be the star of your own movie as you experience the happiness, joy, and fulfillment of living your dream. You can focus on one goal or multiple goals depending on how long you do this meditation for.

3. If you'd like, you can add affirmative prayers to support your visualization!

It's incredibly important to allow the feeling of living your dream to surface. Emotions are energy in motion that interact with the field of infinite potentiality to manifest your material world.

Don't be afraid to let your imagination fly. Your attention should be in the details of your experience. Imagine with all your senses engaged, your heart fully present, and your emotional body open to receive the experience.

When you are truly invested in your creative visualization, there is no separation between you and the experience of what you want as if you have it now. You live it, you experience it, **and it feels amazing!**

5. THE 4 ATTITUDES

The 4 Attitudes are an ancient set of principles that help to align the mind with the soul. Through the 4 Attitudes, you can raise your level of consciousness and connect to the miracle of life.

The 4 Attitudes are as follows:

1. I praise the divine for my life.

2. I thank the divine for my body.

3. The divine loves me.

4. Om shanti.

The Meditation

1. Find a comfortable seat and close your eyes.

2. Let your hands rest comfortably on your knees or in your lap.

3. Silently repeat the 4 Attitudes to yourself for 5 to 20 minutes while focusing on your heart center.

   HELPFUL TIP: I love doing this meditation with mala beads, silently repeating one attitude for each of the 108 mala beads. See page 49 for guidance!

6. MANIFESTATION PRAYER

Manifestation prayer is another powerful way of asking god-source and the universe for what you want.

Write down the 3 things you want the most in your life.

1. _____

2. _____

3. _____

The Meditation

1. Find a comfortable seat and close your eyes.

2. Let your hands rest comfortably on your knees or in your lap.

3. From a heart-centered space, silently repeat the things you want.

4. Then, repeat these words to yourself silently:
"You know what I want. Please give it to me in the path of least resistance. Thank you. Now it is done. It is done. It is done. It is done."

7. WHITE LIGHT MEDITATION

This meditation comes from the tradition of reiki. It floods the body with love and light, helping you to release physical, emotional, and energetic blockages.

The Meditation

1. Find a comfortable seat and close your eyes.

2. Place your right hand on your heart center. Place your left hand on top of your right.

3. Imagine a space a few feet above your crown.

4. As you inhale, imagine that you are breathing in love and light into your crown all the way down to your belly. If it helps, you can visualize a white light or a golden stream of energy as you inhale.

5. On the exhale, feel this beautiful life-force energy radiating to every cell of your being and out the edges of your skin. As you continue with your exhales, feel this loving energy extending farther and farther until it reaches the outer edges of the universe and beyond.

MINDFULNESS & MANTRA MEDITATION

Both mindfulness and mantra meditation serve the same purpose, to still your mind and connect you to the true essence of your being. Because they serve the same purpose, explore each, and then choose your favorite to integrate into your daily spiritual practice.

Mindfulness Meditation

1. Find a comfortable seat and close your eyes.

2. Rest your hands wherever they feel comfortable.

3. Draw your awareness to the natural rhythm of your breath.

4. Continue to observe your breath. If and when a thought arises, it's totally fine. Notice the thought, and then draw your awareness back to your breath. If it helps, you can acknowledge the thought by silently repeating the word "thought" to yourself before returning to your breath.

5. As your meditation continues, notice the space between the inhale and exhale as well as the slowing down of the breath toward the bottom of the exhale before it returns to the inhale.

Mantra meditation is similar to mindfulness meditation except that you will use a mantra for your object of awareness instead of your breath. Here are some mantras to choose from:

Om
Om Shanti
Om Namah Shivaya
I Am Peace
I Am Love
I Am That I Am

A mantra is a sacred sound vibration that focuses and stills the mind. For the purpose of meditation, you needn't concern yourself with knowing the meaning of the mantra.

Mantra Meditation

1. Find a comfortable seat and close your eyes.

2. Rest your hands wherever they feel comfortable.

3. Silently repeat your mantra to yourself. It should be like a gentle whisper.

4. If and when your mind strays away from your mantra to a thought, bodily sensation, or external distraction, that's totally fine. Notice it, and then draw your awareness back to your mantra.

Mantra meditation can also be done using mala beads if you prefer. When you do this, it's called japa. Japa can be done anytime and anywhere!

Japa Meditation

1. Purchase a 108-bead mala. You can wear it around your wrist or neck for easy access.

2. Grasp the bead to the left of the guru bead (bead with the knot) with your thumb and middle finger.

3. Close your eyes if so desired.

4. Slide your thumb and middle finger from bead to bead silently repeating your mantra once for each bead.

5. When you get to the last bead before the guru bead, you can flip the mala around and start again in the opposite direction if you'd like.

MORE ABOUT MEDITATION

Mindfulness and mantra meditation are both forms of concentrative meditation. Concentrative meditation, practiced on a daily basis for 20 minutes, leads to better focus, less anxiety, more creativity, and less stress.

You can think of meditation as a systematic process of training the mind. Essentially, you are building the muscle that allows you to **consciously** choose your state of being every moment of your life regardless of what's happening around you.

Even if your external circumstances remain the same, your reaction to those circumstances will change. You will live every moment with more peace, calm, and equanimity. *This is the gift of meditation.*

It is perfectly natural for thoughts to arise during meditation. Don't fight them. Instead, do your best to be aware of the thoughts as they arise so that you become empowered to draw your attention back to your object of awareness, your breath or a mantra.

As you cultivate mindfulness in your seated meditations, that mindfulness will naturally filter out into your everyday life. When you are mindful of your thoughts and actions, you can consciously choose thoughts and actions that support your goals in life.

On a deeper level, meditation awakens you to your true self. Your true self is the aspect of your being that was never born and will never die. It is eternal, infinite, and one with all of creation. By its very nature, it is pure joy and bliss.

As you awaken to your true self in meditation, the act of sitting and observing your breath or silently repeating a mantra will become such a blissful, joyful experience that you will never want to stop! In this stage of meditation, you will understand that happiness truly does come from within.

HELPFUL TIP: The biggest transformational shift you can make toward creating the life of your dreams is to prioritize meditation and other soul-nurturing activities. Your logical mind wants to be busy all the time, making progress and crossing things off your to-do list. But when you step back from the outside world and make communing with your spirit your number-one priority in life, everything else will start to fall into place.

5 MEDITATION TIPS

1. Do your best to create a sacred space that is solely devoted for meditation. But if you're traveling, know that any place can be turned into a sacred space for meditation simply with your intention.

2. It's best to sit up nice and tall for meditation so that energy is free to rise up and down the spine. But comfort is key. So if you need support for your back, that's fine. If you have an itch, scratch it! If you need to adjust your legs to make yourself more comfortable, go for it!

3. Turn off anything that could be a potential distraction for your meditation. If it helps to set the mood, feel free to light a candle or a stick of incense.

4. The right music can help your mind and body relax into meditation. Check out some of my music recommendations at: www.awakenwithdarren.com.

5. I AM affirmations become incredibly powerful when you are settled into the seat of your soul in deep, heart-centered meditation. Rather than just being positive thoughts, they become statements of truth that vibrate from the core of your being. So feel free to explore your I AM affirmations toward the end of a mindfulness or mantra meditation.

YOGA

Yoga is a moving meditation. By focusing on the breath while moving the body, the mind is stilled.

Yoga can also act as preparation for seated meditation. There are many different types of yoga. Two of the most transformative practices for modern times are hatha yoga and bhakti yoga.

Hatha yoga refers to any type of yoga that involves physical postures. By practicing hatha yoga, you will release tension in the body, strengthen and tone the body, increase flexibility, and most importantly, still the mind.

Bhakti yoga is the yoga of love and devotion. This path usually draws on Hindu gods and goddesses which each represent an aspect of the divine. But any object of devotion that you resonate with, from any religion or spiritual path, is perfectly suited to practice bhakti.

The most popular practice of bhakti yoga is kirtan, the call and response singing of devotional music. The ultimate goal of bhakti yoga is to experience bliss and joy achieved in the devotional surrender to the divine. The divine can be loved as a servant, a friend, a parent, a child, or a lover.

Here are 5 ways you can practice bhakti yoga:

1. Chant songs of praise to the divine either alone or at a kirtan.

2. Set up an altar with a favorite representation of the divine, and offer flowers, fruit, or incense.

3. Meditate on your chosen image of the divine. Visualize the image in your mind's eyes, and concentrate on it while observing your breath.

4. See nature as a manifestation of the divine.

5. Practice japa.

PRANAYAMA

Pranayama means breath control. It facilitates the connection between the breath, the mind, and the emotions.

Here is a simple 7-minute pranayama routine. All of these breathing exercises are done through your nose.

Dirgha (Three-Part Breath) — 3 minutes
Observe a deep breath moving from your belly, into your rib cage, and into your chest. Take a nice slow and controlled exhale in the opposite direction.

Kapalabhati (Breath of Fire) — 1 minute
Inhale slowly. Forcefully exhale while pumping the stomach inwards. The next inhale will happen naturally as this breathing exercise continues for 30 rounds of breath. After 30 rounds of breath, take a few natural breaths, and then do another round of 30.

Nadi Shodhana (Alternate Nostril Breathing) — 3 minutes
With your left hand, place your index and middle finger in-between your brows. Take a normal inhale and exhale. Softly close the right nostril with your ring finger. Inhale slowly into the left nostril. Take a brief pause at the top of the inhale. Softly close the left nostril with your thumb, and exhale through the right nostril. Repeat for 3 minutes then return to observing the natural rhythm of your breath.

YOUR DAILY PRACTICE

Now that you're familiar with several different forms of active meditation, mindfulness and mantra meditation, yoga, and pranayama, it's time to create your own daily spiritual practice routine!

Here is a sample practice...

Morning Routine:

1. Ten minutes of hatha or bhakti yoga

2. Pranayama

3. One or two active meditations

Evening Routine:

1. Fifteen minutes of mindfulness or mantra meditation

Your Daily Practice

Morning Routine:

1. _____

2. _____

3. _____

4. _____

Evening Routine:

1. _____

2. _____

3. _____

4. _____

✻ MORNING & EVENING RITUALS

The most successful people in life have morning and evening rituals that keep them grounded, focused, present, and moving toward their goals. The daily spiritual practices you just created will be an integral part of your daily rituals.

Here is a sample morning ritual:

1. Upon waking, I say out loud, "Today is a sacred day."

2. I immediately do my morning spiritual practice. (The one you just created two pages ago)

3. I have a light, healthy breakfast.

4. I journal for 10 minutes.

5. I take a shower and get dressed.

6. Only then do I use my phone and computer.

Here is a sample evening ritual:

1. I turn off my phone and computer at 10 p.m.

2. I read a personal growth book for 20 minutes.

3. I write in my gratitude journal for 5 minutes.

4. I do my evening daily spiritual practice and then go to sleep.

The discipline of committing to your rituals will act as a bridge between your goals and their accomplishment. It is during this time of stepping back from your life that you create the space for your **dreams** to manifest.

73

Morning Ritual

Write down your morning ritual here!

1. _____
2. _____
3. _____
4. _____
5. _____
6. _____
7. _____
8. _____
9. _____
10. _____

Evening Ritual

Write down your evening ritual here!

1. _____
2. _____
3. _____
4. _____
5. _____
6. _____
7. _____
8. _____
9. _____
10. _____

HEALTHY LIVING HABITS

Healthy living habits are daily and weekly commitments that will keep your mind peaceful, your body healthy, and your spirit strong.

Healthy Living

Create 10 healthy living habits that feel appropriate for you and your unique lifestyle. For inspiration, see the next page!

1. _____
2. _____
3. _____
4. _____
5. _____
6. _____
7. _____
8. _____
9. _____
10. _____

Here are some examples of Healthy Living Habits:

I drink 8 glasses of water every day.

I indulge in an aromatherapy bubble bath every
    Sunday evening.

I check my email a maximum of twice per day.

I limit social media time to 10 minutes per day.

I turn off my phone and computer at 10 p.m. every night.

I take at least 1 nature walk per week.

Here are some more examples of Healthy Living Habits

I get a massage on the last day of every month.

I go to the gym twice per week to nurture my body.

I enjoy 1 hour of television-watching per week.

I take two 60-minute yoga classes per week to still my mind and nurture my body.

At least once a week, I turn the music up loud and dance as if no one is watching!

On the last Sunday of every month I take a technology-free day.

Section 3: The 9 Keys

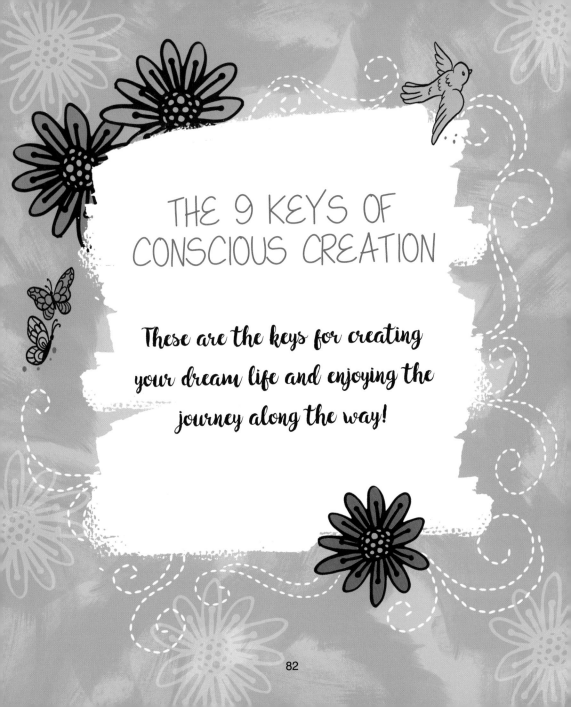

THE 9 KEYS OF CONSCIOUS CREATION

These are the keys for creating your dream life and enjoying the journey along the way!

PRESENCE

Presence is the 1st key to creating your dream life because if you want to step into your power, live your truth, and awaken your full potential, you need to be present to what is here and now.

When you are constantly thinking about a better future, dwelling in the past, overreacting to circumstances around you, or allowing yourself to be distracted in any way from what is actually happening in the now, you are not present.

Presence occurs when you are in an active state of awareness of what is happening in the moment. It is here, in presence, where you make contact with the eternal aspect of your being, your soul.

When you make contact with
your soul, you return home.
Home is your sweet spot.
When you are home, you can
truly enjoy life. You are silent,
present, and aware. Meditation
and other soul-nurturing
activities are the tools that
can bring you home.

The best creative ideas and intuitive insights spring from this sweet spot, the source of stillness within you. From there, you can take relaxed, inspired action that moves you forward toward your dreams.

Meditation doesn't have to be your only tool to bring you into the present moment. Here are some other activities that can help draw your mind into stillness so you can be truly awake to the present moment:

Play with a pet
Sit by a lake and admire nature
Smell flowers
Chant mantras
Play a musical instrument
Create art
Get a massage
Dance
Provide selfless service
Take a yoga class

Present Moment

What brings YOU into the present moment?

1. _____

2. _____

3. _____

4. _____

5. _____

6. _____

7. _____

8. _____

9. _____

10. _____

THE EGO

The ego is where we form thoughts and opinions about ourselves, our abilities, our experiences, and our relationships with others.

The **ego and presence** are highly interconnected. A healthy ego encourages presence and lovingly supports our highest vision and purpose. But the ego can also take us out of presence, away from our dreams, and cause unnecessary suffering in our lives.

Here are some things the ego loves to do:

The ego loves to make excuses for not moving confidently towards our dreams.
The ego loves to judge a moment as being good or bad.
The ego loves to label people, places, and things.
The ego loves to say, "I should've, would've, could've."
The ego loves to worry about the future.
The ego loves to complain about the present moment.
The ego loves to procrastinate because of fear and outdated belief systems.
The ego loves to insist that happiness can only exist tomorrow.
The ego loves to judge others who think and act differently.

When you begin to observe the thoughts of the ego from a state of presence, becoming witness to them in the same way you would observe clouds in the sky, you start to awaken from the dream of the ego that has controlled your life and held you back from living the life you want and deserve.

If a thought is loving, supportive, and helpful, then you know the ego is aligned with your soul's purpose. If not, then you know that thought needs to be replaced with a more positive, loving, nurturing thought.

The best way to treat your ego is the same way you would treat a child, with love and compassion. True love is all-encompassing and embraces all the facets of our beings. So instead of viewing your ego as the enemy, embrace your ego as your friend and teacher. Accept that it is part of your being. Your job is not to erase it, but rather to gently coax it into serving your soul.

HELPFUL TIP: When you observe a thought or thought stream that is not serving you, lovingly question it. Ask yourself, "Is this the truth?" The truth springs from your I AM presence, the all-loving infinite intelligence of your spirit.

FUN EXERCISE

Next time you catch your ego acting up with a negative thought about yourself, replace that thought with this positive affirmation: "The truth is that I AM fill in the blank."

SYNCHRONICITY

As you progress with your meditation practice, spend more time in presence, align your ego with your soul, and take inspired action, more and more synchronicity will appear in your life.

A synchronicity is any life experience that lets you know you're on the right path. Often, a synchronicity will be an event or experience that leads you closer to achieving a goal.

Ironically, synchronicity often happens when we least expect it. This is where "the art of letting go" comes into play. After you've planted the seeds of growth through your meditations and action steps, have faith and believe that it will be done. Then watch as miracles occur in your life!

Each **synchronicity** is a stepping stone that will lead to the full manifestation of what you want. Allow the mystery to unfold, and **enjoy the journey.**

101

Synchronicity

Keep track of all the synchronicities
that occur in your life here!

1. _____

2. _____

3. _____

4. _____

5. _____

6. _____

7. _____

8. _____

9. _____

10. _____

ALIGNMENT

You don't have to say yes to everything that is offered to you in life. Every time you say no to something that's not part of your highest vision, you create the space for what you do want to come into your life.

Always remember, you are a divine being worthy of receiving everything that you want to make yourself truly happy and satisfied!

Embrace stepping stones that keep you on the path toward accomplishing your goals. But don't be afraid to take that leap of faith when necessary by letting go of what no longer serves you.

Letting go of people, places, and things that no longer serve your highest and best interests requires **courage and bravery.** But your dream life is waiting for you, so be brave!

Letting go

What are you willing to let go of today?

I am willing to let go of _____.

I am willing to let go of _____.

I am willing to let go of _____.

FAITH

If you watch a flower grow, it might not seem as if it's growing at all. But if you plant the seed and give it sunlight and water, the infinite intelligence of the seed will form a beautiful flower in its own time.

There is an infinite intelligence at work in your life, too. Even if you can't see your destination, maintain your vision and keep the faith. Faith is imperative if you want to create your dream life.

Live with the excitement
that what you want is
coming toward you and that
it is going to come into your
life in the very near future.
This expectancy will put you
into alignment with that
which you seek.

PRAYER

Prayer can play an important part in creating your dream life. If the concept of prayer resonates with you, pray spontaneously whenever you feel like it, or add it to your morning or evening ritual.

Prayer does not have to be associated with religion. You can think of prayer as communicating the desires of your heart to any form of the divine you resonate with.

Prayer should be like an intimate conversation with a good friend who is always eager to listen and help. As long as it's heartfelt, that's all that matters.

Prayer will help you feel *more connected* to source and will invoke powerful energies to help you manifest the desires of your heart. Be patient with your prayers. Some prayers take time to be answered.

LOVE & SELFLESS SERVICE

You were put here for a purpose. That purpose is to express the love that you are. The greatest joys in life are found by being of service to others. So it's important not only to focus on what you want, but also on what you have to give.

The intention of utilizing your gifts to impact the lives of others in a beneficial way is the most honorable intention you can have. This is the path of selfless service and is the most direct path to true fulfillment.

True service flows from the recognition that the same source within you flows through all living beings. This source is present regardless of a person's race, religion, color, or belief system.

As you move forward toward creating your dream life, nurture your gifts, share them with the world, and practice as many small random acts of kindness as you can on a daily basis.

My Impact in The World

Write down 10 valuable ways in which
you will impact others by achieving your goals.
Utilize this list as a daily reminder of why it's so
important that you stay driven to succeed.

1. _____

2. _____

3. _____

4. _____

5. _____

6. _____

7. _____

8. _____

9. _____

10. _____

APPRECIATION

As you move from your head to your heart and experience more presence in your life, you will come to understand that all of life is a miracle. Every moment is a gift that should be cherished and enjoyed.

Don't buy into the myth that you will only be happy and satisfied when you achieve your goals. Yes, achieving your goals and living your dream life will be totally awesome. But happiness and satisfaction can also be found in the present moment by tuning into the true essence of your being.

Each new "now moment" offers you the possibility of fulfilling the purpose of creation, which is to give and receive love. These opportunities often appear in the moments that we label as ordinary. By being present to them, they become extraordinary.

When you find contentment wherever you are, you create an energetic shift that opens up new doorways into future timelines that will be filled with even more contentment!

ADVANCED PRACTICE

Do your best to give thanks for bad times as well as the good times. From every experience, there is always wisdom to be learned. Often in life, it's the most painful experiences that allow us to grow into who we are meant to be.

BEING HUMAN

You incarnated into a physical form. It's impossible to take the humanness out of your being. You are not meant to do things perfectly. Accept your imperfections.

Practice ahimsa, the path of nonviolence. Treat yourself and others with unconditional love and compassion. When you catch yourself speaking badly about yourself or thinking badly about another, pause and return to your default setting. Your default setting is love.

At least once a day, remind yourself of this simple truth: Right here and right now, I am making a beneficial impact in the world just being who I am as a friend, a colleague, a mother, a father, a sibling, a grandparent, or in any other way that I am serving.

Kindness

Take a moment to remind yourself of all the beautiful ways in which you are serving the world and those around you RIGHT NOW. Be proud of that.

1. _____
2. _____
3. _____
4. _____
5. _____
6. _____
7. _____
8. _____
9. _____
10. _____

Section 4:
A Little More
Inspiration

RAISE YOUR VIBRATION

Everything is energy and every living thing is vibrating at a particular frequency. When you raise your vibration, you experience more love, connect with your angels and guides, and move into alignment with that which you seek.

Here are 10 ways to raise your vibration, many of which you have been introduced to already

1. Be mindful of your thoughts. Your thoughts are the seeds that shape your reality.
2. Appreciate the simple things in life.
3. Allow yourself to feel and release emotions.
4. Be conscious of the foods you eat.
5. Be conscious of what you read, listen to, and watch. You have every right to choose to give your attention to things that make you feel good!
6. Drink lots of water.
7. Meditate often!
8. Practice as many random acts of kindness as you can every day.
9. Exercise a few days a week.
10. Spend as much time as you can in nature. Mother Nature vibrates at the same frequency as a healthy human being. That's why it feels so good, nurturing, and peaceful to be in nature!

YOU CAN DO IT!

Most people wait for that perfect moment to begin living for their dreams. But that perfect moment never comes. NOW is your moment, and NOW is your time. Whatever you seek in life, step toward it now!

As you go about your life, prioritize. Choose to focus mostly on the activities that are related to achieving your most important goals. Prioritizing is a great opportunity to dramatically transform your life.

It's important to remember that the highest possibilities for your life arise in the midst of silence, not from a busy, overwhelmed, overthinking mind. Overthinking and overanalyzing block the gateway between you and your true self. If you experience more peace and presence in your life, everything else will flourish.

Failure and obstacles are part of life. As an inventor, Edison made 1,000 unsuccessful attempts at inventing the light bulb before succeeding. Don't let failures and setbacks get in your way of achieving your dreams. Success is always just around the corner.

Congrats! You've now completed all your fun work. My wish for you is that you journey onward to experience a wonderful life filled with peace, happiness, and all that your heart desires. I will leave you with a channeled quote from my spirit guides:

Courage is about not knowing how it will go, but doing it anyway because you know you have to, because there is an inner urge that pulls you forward toward it, and you know you must do it. That is your spirit speaking. It is the strength of your spirit that says, "Let's take the next step even though it is scary."

Many blessings, Darren

About the Author

Darren Marc is a celebrated musician, reiki master, intuitive life coach, and yogi. He has written articles for *L.A Yoga Magazine* and *4Health Magazine*. His vision is to inspire and awaken joy, divine connection, wisdom, and love in all. To access bonus book materials, visit: *www.awakenwithdarren.com.*

About the Illustrator

Joan Coleman, an avid artist since childhood and a professional artist for over 10 years, is a talented and versatile children's book illustrator. Her company, Ink Wonderland, works with authors and publishers all across the U.S.A. and around the world. Visit Joan at her website: *www.inkwonderland.com.*

48065380R10104